THE BUSHCRAFT HANDBOOKS

BUSH HUTMAKING

Illustrations by the Author

Richard H. Graves

The Bushcraft Handbooks
Bush Hutmaking

This Edition Copyright © 2013 by Palmer River Publishing

Cover, Graphics and Layout by: Palmer River Publishing

All rights reserved. No part of this book may be reproduced in any form by any electronic or mechanical means including photocopying, recording, or information storage and retrieval without permission in writing from the author.

ISBN-13: 978-1484812624
ISBN-10: 148481262X

About The Author

The author of "The Bushcraft Handbooks", Richard Graves, is a member of the Irish literary family of that name. A veteran of the Great War campaigns in the Dardenelles and the Western Front, the author became passionate about the bush at an early age. As an enthusiastic bushwalker, skier and pioneer of white-water canoeing, he foresaw how a knowledge of bushcraft could save lives in the Second World War. To achieve this end, he initiated and led the Australian Jungle Rescue Detachment, assigned to the Far East American Air Force. This detachment of 60 specially selected A.I.F. soldiers successfully effected more than 300 rescue missions, most of which were in enemy-held territory in New Guinea, without failure of a mission or loss of a man.

An essential preliminary for rescue was survival, and it was for this purpose that the notes for these books were written. These notes were later revised and prepared for a School in Bushcraft which has been operating for several years and continues to provide valuable instruction to Servicemen embarking overseas on active service in Korea and Malaya.

Bushcraft

As far as is known, "The Bushcraft Handbooks" are unique. There is nothing quite like them, nor is any collection of published bushcraft knowledge as comprehensive.

The term "Bushcraft" is used because "woodcraft" commonly means either knowledge of local fauna and flora or else is associated with the blood-sports of hunting and shooting. "The Bushcraft Handbooks" include a volume on traps and snares, but these are purposely-designed to be completely ineffective for native animals which are insect enters or grazers. These traps have been included because they would only be effective in catching predatory animals such as cats and dogs which have taken to the bush, and other "pest" creatures such as feral swine or goat.

"Bushcraft" describes the activity of how to make use of natural materials found locally in any area. It includes many of the skills used by primitive man, and to these are added "white man" skills necessary for survival, such as time and direction, and the provision of modern "white man" comforts as illustrated in the volume on bush campcraft.

The practice of bushcraft develops in an individual a remarkable ability to adapt quickly to a changing environment. Because this is so, the activity is a valuable counter to the over-specialisation so prevalent in today's society, and is particularly significant in youth training and character-moulding work.

INTRODUCTION to the BUSHCRAFT HANDBOOKS

THE PRACTICE OF BUSHCRAFT shows many unexpected results. The five senses are sharpened, and consequently the joy of being alive is greater.

The individual's ability to adapt and improvise is developed to a remarkable degree. This in turn leads to increased self-confidence.

Self-confidence, and the ability to adapt to a changing environment and to overcome difficulties, is followed by a rapid improvement in the individual's daily work. This in turn leads to advancement and promotion.

Bushcraft, by developing adaptability, provides a broadening influence, a necessary counter to offset the narrowing influence of modern specialisation.

For this work of bushcraft all that is needed is a sharp cutting implement: knife, axe or machete. The last is the most useful. For the work, dead materials are most suitable. The practice of bushcraft conserves, and does not destroy, wild life.

R.H.G.
April, 1952

CONTENTS

About The Author ... iii
Bushcraft ... iii

INTRODUCTION to the BUSHCRAFT HANDBOOKS ... v

BUSH HUTMAKING ... 1

Thatched Huts ... 2
Design ... 3
Sectional Lean-To Huts ... 5
Permanent Lean-To Huts ... 7
Pyramidal Huts ... 8
Long Hut ... 9
Step-By-Step Construction of a Circular Hut ... 11
Poles and Structures ... 14
Bracing ... 14
Doors and Windows ... 15
Tree Swinging Shelter ... 16
Thatching Materials ... 18
Thatching Methods ... 19
Principles of Watershed in Thatching ... 20
Sewn Thatching ... 21
Stick Thatch ... 22
Tuft Thatching ... 22
Stalk Thatch ... 23
Split Stalk Thatch ... 24
Woven Thatch ... 24
Sewn Batten Thatch ... 25
Ridge Thatching ... 25
Sewn Ridge Thatching ... 26
Crown Ridge Thatch ... 27
Guttering ... 27
Flashing ... 28

Rammed Earth ... 28
Foundations ... 29
Soil Qualities for Rammed Earth ... 29
Forms ... 31

Log Cabins ... 33

Materials for Lashings ... 34

Barks ... 35

Special Knots ... 35

Sedges and Bulrushes ... 35

Joining Green Materials ... 36

Wall Pegs ... 37

BUSH HUTMAKING

Little skill is needed to make a comfortable, thatched, weatherproof hut using only material locally available.

Such huts can be expected to have a useful service life of 4 to 6 years without maintenance. With maintenance, such as renewing lashings, and repairs to ridge thatch, the life is anything up to 20 years.

Where rammed earth is used for walls, the life of the structure is indeterminate. Many earth wall buildings have stood undamaged for hundreds of years.

The building of a thatched hut from local materials is a creative exercise. Design must provide for the anticipated weather conditions. Finding suitable materials almost anywhere presents no problem, but considerable organisation may be required to collect the material. For the actual structure and thatching, good teamwork is required.

The final hut, with its promise of long periods of protection and shelter, is the result of combination of head work and hands. With this comes the inward reward of having created a weather-proof hut out of nothing except the natural materials garnered from the surrounding area.

Circular hut 20 feet diameter at ground; no nails or manmade materials used in its construction. Time of erection, 12 to 18 man hours. Left half is thatched with palm leaves—right half thatched with eucalypt branches. Shortly after erection there was 4½ inches of rain in 75 minutes. The inside of the hut was completely dry after this terrific drenching.

Thatched Huts

The making of huts and shelters for occasional or continuous use from exclusively local materials and without the aid of any man-made equipment is not difficult. In place of nails, lashings, either of vine, bark strips or other fibrous material are used. Framework is of round poles. Weatherproof roofing is provided by thatching with long grass, ferns, reeds, palm leaves, sea weeds, bark sheets, split shingles or even sods of clayey turf.

The material you will use depends on what there is in your vicinity. The shape, size and details of your hut are governed by the length of your occupation; the number of people that have to be sheltered; the local climatic conditions against which you want shelter; and, of course, the time available for construction.

If there are one or two to be sheltered for a few nights only in a temperate climate, a simple lean-to thatched shelter will suffice and this can be built in one to three hours, but if there are eight or ten in your party and they require shelter for a few months against cold and bad weather, then a semipermanent hut complete with doors, windows, and a fireplace for heating, and built-in bunks will be required, and to do this properly might take two or three days.

It is assumed that a good knife, hatchet or axe is available and that the workers are willing. The structures shown here are merely examples of what can be done. When it comes to planning your hut, you are your own architect and your own builder. If there are several people in the party, organise the labour so that no hands are idle—have one or two fellows cutting poles, another carrying them to the site, a fourth stripping bark for lashings (see the Bushcraft Handbook titled "Ropemaking"), and set the others gathering material for thatching.

Collect all the material for your structure before you start to build, stack it in orderly piles where it will be most convenient. Your main structure poles in one pile; your battens for thatching in another pile; your bark strips or vines shredded down for immediate use; and your thatching material neatly stacked in several piles close to the work.

When you are ready to start building, have every man on the site. Organise the labour of erection of the main framework, and then break your team up into small gangs for lashing on battens and completing details of framework. By this means you will save hours of labour and you will succeed in building a better hut.

There is nothing to it really, except intelligence. Plan and organise to keep everybody's fingers busily engaged.

Design

There are three main designs of huts: a simple lean-to hut, suitable for fine warm weather; an enclosed pyramidal hut, suitable for cold, inclement conditions; and a long hut, which if open is suitable for mild climates, or if completely walled is suitable for cold conditions.

Refinements such as doors (yes, doors that swing on hinges) and windows may be added to suit your pleasure. And when your hut is completed, then there is the all important matter of furnishing it—but first let us look at what the backwoods man can build for his new season camp.

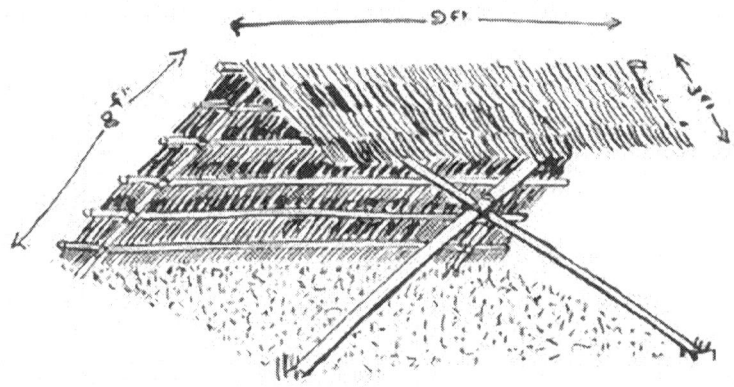

This would be suitable for a short summer shelter for two fellows. It can be put up in one to three hours.

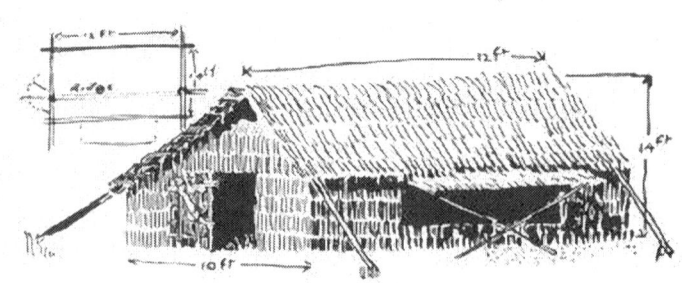

This long hut, about twelve feet by ten feet wide, will house five to twelve men, depending on the bunking arrangements, and can be built in about 40 man hours.

This pyramidal hut, 14 feet square inside the 5 ft. high walls, is comfortable, and an excellent cold weather camp for from eight to sixteen men, according to the bunking arrangements. It can be put up in about 20 man hours.

Sectional Lean-To Huts

Small one and two man lean-to huts can be easily constructed in an hour or two by making and thatching two or three frames which are from seven to nine feet in length and three feet six to four feet deep.

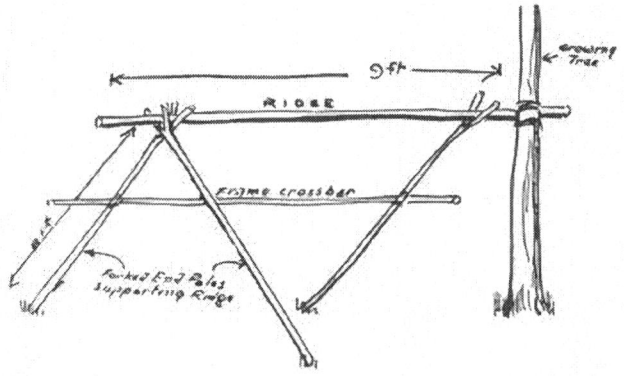

Framework for Sectional Lean-to Shelter

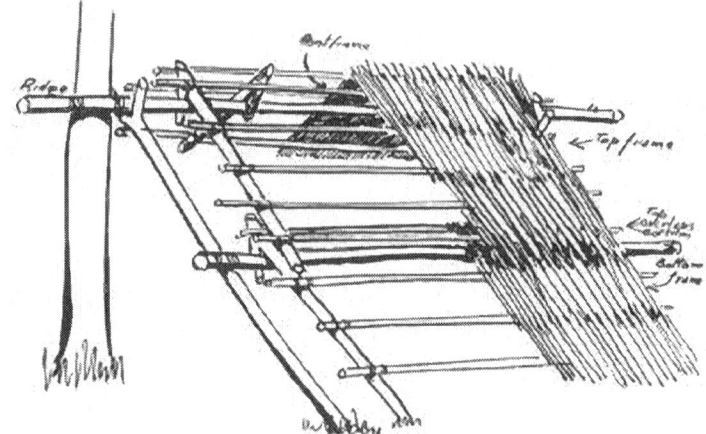

Three Thatched Sections attach to Crossbar and Ridge.

These frames, built of battens, are lashed on to two fork sticks. The forks are in the form of hooks at the upper end. The framework for these one or two man shelters is simple to construct.

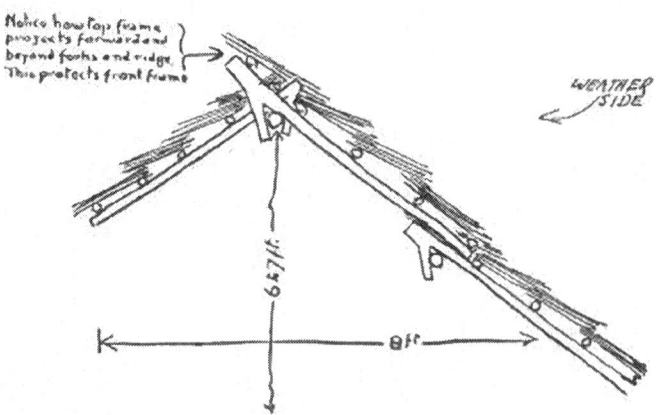

Assembly on framework of sections.

Note how top of top frame projects forward beyond fork and ridge. This protects front frame, and saves the work of ridge thatching. If raised bunks (see Chapter 3) are being put in, it is advisable to have bottom of thatch about 1'6" to 2' above ground. This raises ridge height to 1' to 1'6" and side poles become 10 to 11 ft. instead of 8 to 9 ft.

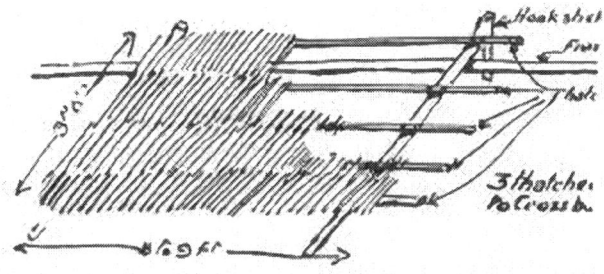

Section of assembly.

Permanent Lean-To Huts

The permanent lean-to hut using a tree for bracing is simple and quick to erect.

Cutaway section of frame for hut sited between two saplings

The ridge pole is raised against the tree by means of the two end forked poles to the required height, between eight to ten feet, depending on the width. The end forked poles should be at an angle of not less than 45 deg. If the length of ridge is more than 10 to 12 feet, it is advisable to put in another one or two forked poles about halfway along.

On to the end forked poles lash a crossbar ("A") and lash it again to the upright tree. This crossbar has lashed to its front end a pole ("B") connecting and lashed to the ridge, and also the front eaves pole ("C"), and also the front thatching battens.

Thatching battens are lashed on to the two rear forks. The distance apart for the thatching battens varies: it may be anything from 6 to 12 in., depending on the length of thatching material being used. A general guide is that battens should be distant about one-fourth of the average length of the thatching material.

An upright in the form of a light fork may be placed under the front corners to the front eave pole. Wall thatch battens are lashed horizontally from the rear forked poles to this upright to wall in the ends of the hut. Wall pegs are driven in along the rear at whatever height is required and to these wall pegs thatching battens are also lashed.

Forked poles should be not less than 3 to 4 in. in diameter-thatching battens from 1 to 2 in. Ridge pole about 3 to 4 in.

Use dry timber or dead timber wherever possible. It is lighter to handle and its use avoids destruction of the bush. When making wall pegs bevel off the head—they will then drive into the ground without splitting.

Pyramidal Huts

The pyramidal hut, having a square base, is particularly useful where it is desired to make the fullest possible use of wall and floor space.

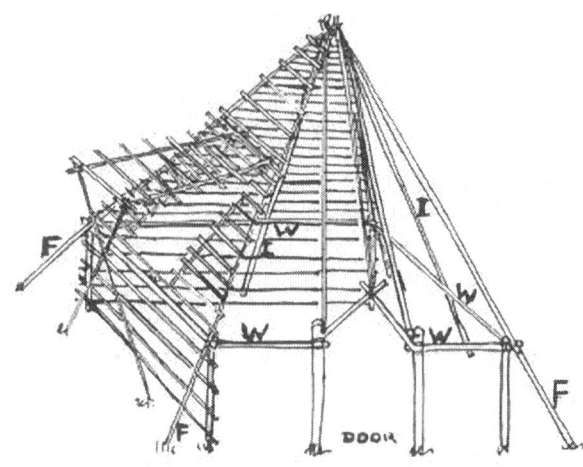

Pyramidal hut, showing window frame, thatch battens and main structure.

BUSH HUTMAKING

W — WALL RAIL
I — INTERMEDIATE POLES.
F — FORKED CORNER POLES.

The construction is very much the same for a circular hut except for the intermediate poles. Erection time is considerably less for the pyramidal hut. In this type of hut it is more efficient, when lashing on thatching battens, to make one lashing at each corner secure the two thatching battens, and when the span between fork poles becomes six feet or less to lash only to the corner poles, omitting the lashing to the intermediate poles. If the span between corner poles is greater than six feet it is necessary to lash battens to the intermediate poles.

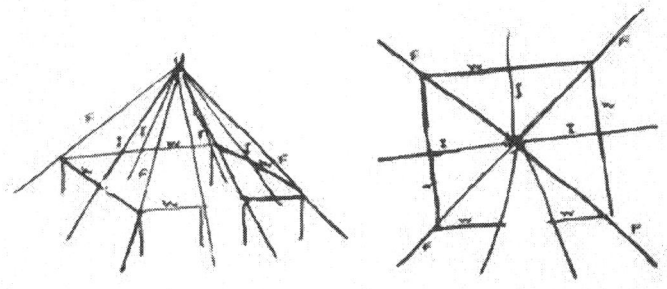

F — FORK POLES
I — INTERMEDIATE POLES
W — WALL POLES

Long Hut

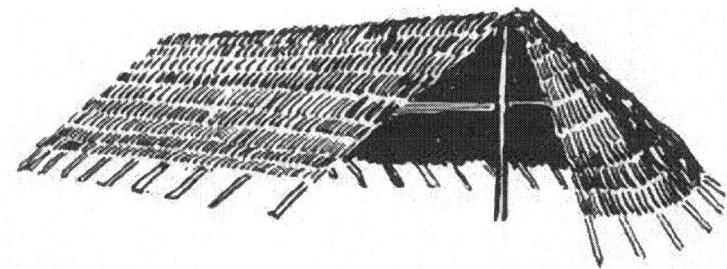

Hut, sixty feet long twenty feet wide, by sixteen feet high, built by five men in four days.

The end portion of this structure is basically the same as one-half section of the pyramid hut.

The length can be extended to any required distance by prolonging the ridge pole and using additional supporting fork poles. If the ridge is extended and in two or more lengths, these should be lashed together, and it is advisable to notch the ridge so it will sit snugly in the interlocking forks.

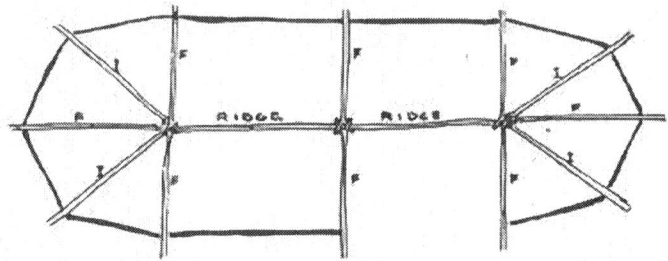

Plan of Long Hut. Intermediate poles required if fork poles are more than 6ft. apart.

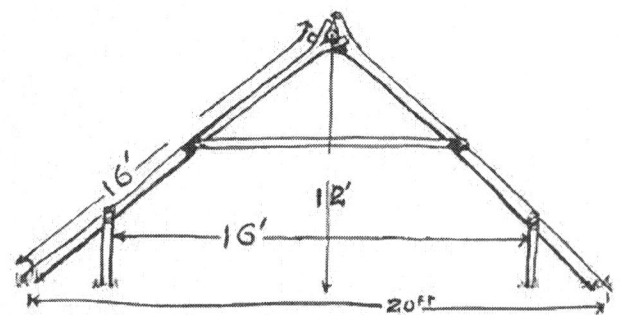

When the span is more than 12 ft. lash collar ties on to forks and intermediate poles.

Wall pegs are driven in at a convenient wall height and thatching battens are lashed down. Refinements such as "lift up" sections for light and ventilation can be added if required.

BUSH HUTMAKING

Step-By-Step Construction of a Circular Hut

1) First Construction: 30 minutes after start-off with four men on the job. Note three forked poles to which have been lashed two rafters each, also entrance ridge and entrance poles with wall poles in position.

2) 1 Hour After Start: The basic structure is completed, a start is made with the thatch battens and wall battens, the door fork is swung.

(3) Lashing on the thatching battens to the rafters. Note how the lower battens must be strong enough to bear a man's weight.

(4) One and a half hours after start: Thatching battens are nearly all lashed on, door is complete, ready for thatching.

(5) Two and a half hours after start: The door is completely thatched, and the thatching is well under way on the roof.

(6) Two and a half hours after start: Three rows of roof thatch laid. The hut, which was 15 ft. diameter from wall to wall, was completed one hour later, or three and a half hours after the start. No nails or purchased materials were used. This hut would be serviceable and weather-proof for six to ten years.

Poles and Structures

All slopes to be completely waterproof should be not less than 45 deg. (although a 40 deg. slope will shed water). A slope that is 45 deg. is useful and will give good headroom. To work out the most efficient size of poles for main structure it is advisable to discover first the length of pole required and then the approximate diameter, excluding bark. It will be found that the proportion of spread to pole length at 45 deg. slope is as 4 to 3 between base of poles.

Example: If spread at base of poles is 20 ft., then pole length to ridge or crown of hut will be 15 ft. This proportion is constant and wall space or height is not allowed for in the calculations. In general, a wall height of 3 ft. to 4 ft. is sufficient.

Diameter of timber inside bark can be roughly calculated by allowing a minimum of 1 inch diameter at butt for each four to five feet of length. Thus, if a pole is 10 ft. in length, the diameter of wood clear of bark at butt should be not less than 2½ ins. or, if the pole is 20 ft. long, the diameter at butt should be not less than 5 ins.

If the span is relatively wide, or the timber used relatively light, it is advisable to strengthen the structure and prevent sagging or inward bending of the main poles by putting cross ties or collar ties so that the thrust or weight is thrown from one pole on to the pole opposite.

Bracing

Similarly with bracings, if long huts or lean-to type of huts are being built and there is no strong support, such as a growing tree, it is advisable to lash in diagonal braces that extend if possible from ground at one end to ridge at the other end. These bracings will make even a light hut quite storm-proof.

Doors and Windows

Refinements such as doors and windows are completely practical in thatch huts, and very little extra work is involved. Windows are simply two (or three) forked sticks cut off short below the fork and with one long end projecting.

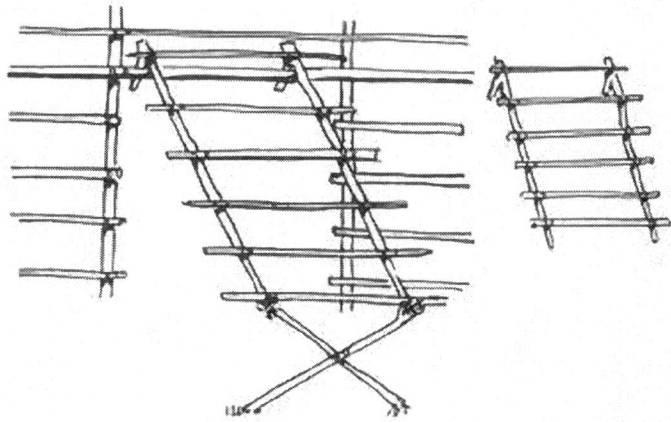

Window frames hook on to thatch batten above window opening.

Thatch battens are lashed to these fork sticks and the framework is lifted up and hung on to one of the thatch battens of the hut. In the general thatching of the hut this window space beneath the windows is left unthatched and the window frame is thatched as a complete unit. It is advisable to leave the window frame rather wider than the opening. It can be propped open at the bottom and still preserve a fair slope. If the window is very wide it is advisable to use three fork sticks. There should be at least six inches overlap of the window and roof thatch at the sides. The loose ends of the thatching above the window frames should be allowed to come directly on to the window thatch, and should completely cover sewing of the top thatching of the window frame.

Doors, if required, are similar to the gate fame shown, but with two uprights lashed across the fork. To these two uprights the horizontal thatching battens are secured.

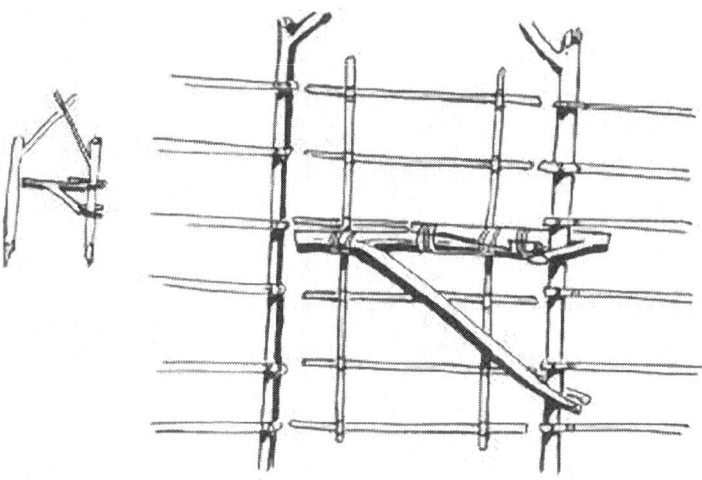

The hinging of the door frame is obtained by a combination of hook and fork.

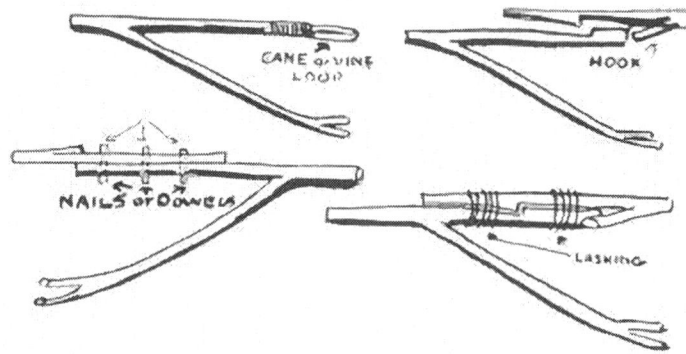

There are several means whereby the door hinge can be assembled.

Tree Swinging Shelter

In swampy country, or in areas which are badly snake infested, a very simple swinging bunk can be made by one man in a day.

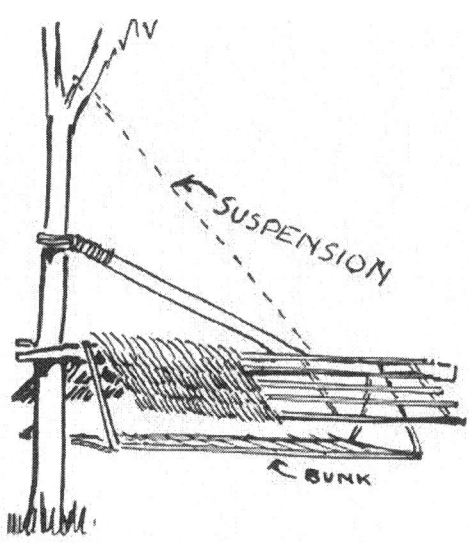

The forked frame stick must be very strong, both at the fork on the tree and at the main juncture. Either a cane or vine loop or a hook may be used at the top section. It is also advisable to have a vine or cane rope from the extreme end of the main frame to as high up in the tree as it is practical to reach for additional suspension.

The frame poles for thatch battens are lashed separately with a square lashing to the bottom of the forked frame stick, and, in order to give rigidity, a short cross stick is lashed horizontally to each of the opposite sides of the frame poles.

When thatching, thatch one row on one side, and then the row on the opposite side. This will help to strengthen the framework and keep it correctly balanced.

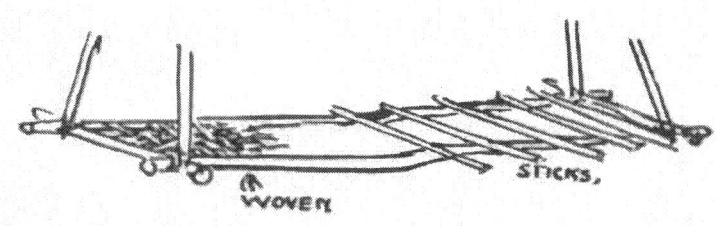

The bunk is made separately.

The main frame of the bunk is simply four poles lashed together to form a rectangle about three feet by seven. The space between the poles to form the bunk proper can be either woven or made with crossed sticks as for the camp bed (see the volume titled "Bush Campcraft").

Thatching Materials

Materials suitable for thatching range from long grass, reeds, rushes; most of the long stalked ferns, such as bracken, etc.; palm leaves of all types, and, as a last resource, many pliant leafy branches.

Long grass and reeds are most satisfactory when used dry or partly dry. It is advisable if you are going to use these materials to cut and stook them first so that they may get a chance to season before being used on the roof.

There are two good reasons for this: first is that in drying out most of these materials, if green and exposed to hot sun, tend to shrink on one side and turn and curl in shrinking, so reducing the coverage value for thatching. The other is the general tendency of all green materials to shrink, and therefore the thatching stitches become loose, and the thatch may slip from the stitches and be blown away in the first breeze.

When the materials are well seasoned the stitches will not slacken because there is very little shrinkage, and the thatch will stay down securely.

With most of the bracken ferns it is advisable to thatch with the material green, and sew it down very tightly. This also applies if you are forced by circumstances to use green branches. These do not make a very efficient thatch and their use is not recommended except in emergency.

In a general way, the use of bracken and reeds for thatching is doing a very good service to the land generally. Bracken is injurious to cattle, and reeds choke watercourses, so that removing these two pests and putting them to practical use is quite a good thing to do.

If branches of trees or shrubs are to be used, seek out a dead branch with some of the leaves still on it. Shake the branch. If the leaves immediately fall from it, the material is almost useless and will only serve you for a day or so. If the leaves withstand this shaking, the plant will probably serve your purpose fairly effectively. Some trees and shrubs drop their leaves within a few hours of being cut. Such are useless.

The palm leaves are best used for thatching when they are dead. You will find great quantities lying under the palms and these are excellent material. They may be brittle and inclined to break if you start collecting them in the middle of a hot summer day.

The best time to collect dead palm for your thatching is either early in the morning when the leaves are softened' by the overnight dew, or after rain. It is always advisable to wet the leaves down before you start sewing them on the thatching battens. This damping down softens the brittle leaves, makes them lie flat, and ensures that you get a better coverage.

Thatching Methods

There are almost as many different methods of thatching as there are different materials. Each different method has its own peculiar advantage and applications for certain types of material.

The methods you are most likely to find of use are either to sew the thatch on to the thatch battens, which is called "Sewn Thatching," or to tuft the material on in bundles, which, appropriately, is called "Tuft Thatching."

Instead of sewing on to the battens you may find it more convenient to tie a pliant stick on to the thatching batten at convenient intervals, using the pressure of this stick tightly tied to the thatch batten to hold the thatch material secure. This is called "Stick Thatching."

There are also several methods by which the thatching materials may be secured to the thatching battens on the ground, and these thatching battens are then laid on to the framework, overlapping like long tiles.

Or with some of the palms the palm stalk itself may be used either as the thatch batten, or to hold the palm leaf itself in the desired position. All these methods are self explanatory, and briefly dealt with on the following pages.

Principles of Watershed in Thatching

Thatching may be either for shade or to give protection against rain. Thatching for shade presents no problems. If the thatch is thick enough to break up the sun's rays, that is all that is required.

Thatching for protection against rain or, under certain conditions, wind, will be effective only if certain principles are observed. It is interesting to watch the behaviour of drops of water on thatch. The drops run down the topmost strands, until they come to the very end of the blade of grass or other material. There the drop gathers size and, when it is big enough, and heavy enough, it falls off and on to the blade immediately beneath.

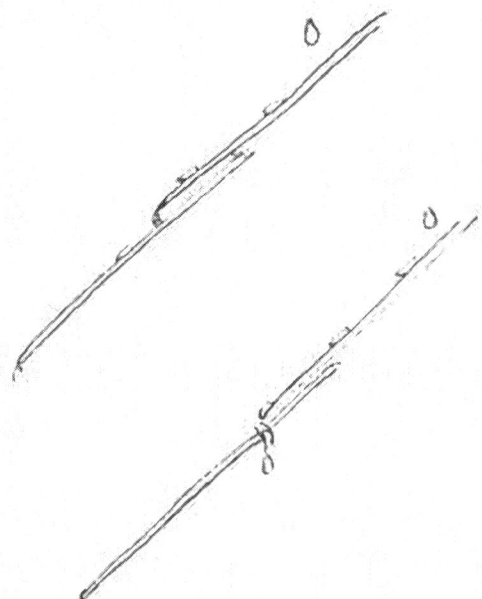

If the stitching interrupts the smooth continued course of the water droplets, then the water will follow the stitching because it is at a steeper angle. It will creep along the stitch and when it reaches the lowest point, on the underside of the thatching batten, the drop will gradually build up until it becomes too heavy to ream in on the sewing material. Then you will complain that the "thatching leaks". Thatch will never leak if the stitching is properly covered.

It is this quality of "coverage" rather than thickness

which makes a thatch waterproof. Windproofing lies largely in the "tightness" and thickness of the thatching.

Sewn Thatching

Stitch at bottom of first thatch on lowest thatching batten. The second layer must overlay the stitching of the first row and include the top section of the underneath layer in the actual stitch. It is better to have each layer held by three rows of stitching. The stitching of every row MUST be completely covered by the free ends of the next layer above it.

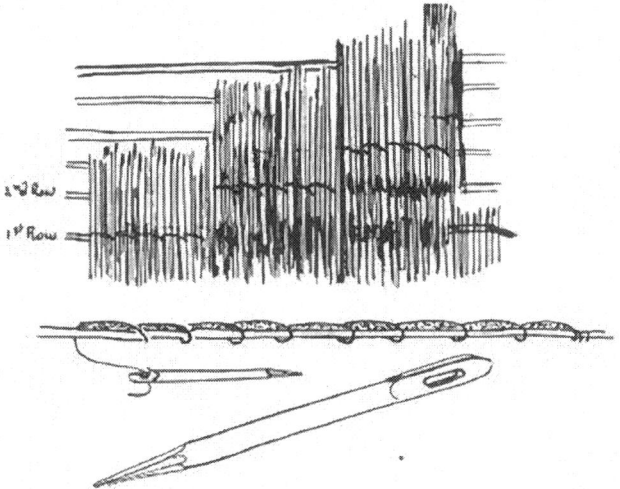

To sew thatching make a thatching needle by cutting a dead, straight grained stick one inch thick and about 18 inches long. Sharpen one end and rub it fairly smooth on a stone. Narrow the other end till it is about one quarter of an inch thick, but the full width of the stick. This end should be flattened for about three inches.

About two inches from the end cut an eye carefully through the flat side. This eye should be about one quarter inch wide and at least half an inch long.

Lay the thatching material with the butts towards the roof and the lower end on the lowest batten. Secure one end of the sewing material with a timber hitch to the thatching batten, thread the other end through the eye of the thatching needle and sew in the ordinary manner to the thatching batten. To avoid holes where the sewing may tend to bunch the thatching together, pass the needle through the thatch at the angle indicated in the sketch and push thatch over the crossing of the stitches.

Stick Thatch

With this stick thatch, ties about two feet apart are fastened on to the thatching batten. The thatching stick is tied at one end, the thatching material placed under it, and when the tie, fixed on the thatching batten is reached, the stick is tied down, thus binding the thatching to the batten. This method of securing thatching is useful when long lengths of material for sewing are not readily available.

The overlapping and general principles of sewn thatching are followed.

Tuft Thatching

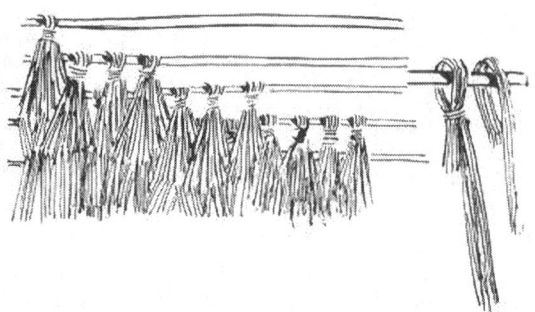

This method is excellent if the material is fairly long, say, two or three feet, and pliable. It is very suitable for reeds and sedges. The thatching material is gathered into small sheaves about an inch or so thick. The butt end is bent over the thatching batten, and a few strands are then twisted round the sheaf a few times and pushed through the bunched up material to hold the end secure. The tuft is then slipped along the thatching batten to lie alongside the preceding tuft. This thatch makes a very neat job from inside. It is secure in all weather, and requires no tying material. If sedge or sword grasses are being used it is advisable to put a pair of socks or gloves on your hands to avoid cuts.

It is important that the long free ends overlap the two or three preceding rows. Do not push the tufts up too tight. There can be about half an inch or more between the bent-over ends on the thatching battens. This open space will be covered by the free ends on the next row.

Stalk Thatch

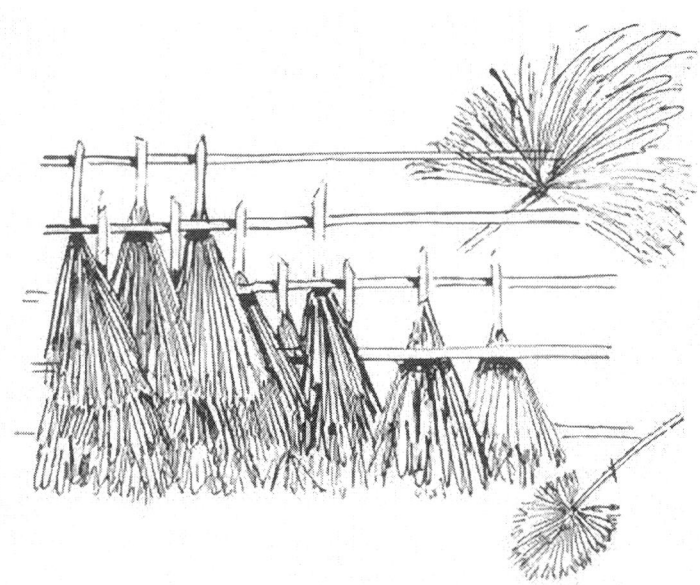

This method is very quick to apply and quite efficient. It is suitable for either the plicate type of palm leaf (as shown above) or the pinnate type (shown overleaf). The stalks are simply woven between the thatch battens. The natural bend forced on the stalks will exert sufficient pressure to hold the leaves securely in position. This is the quickest and easiest of all thatching methods, and quite efficient if the palm leaves are well bunched and have a good overlap to give watershed.

Split Stalk Thatch

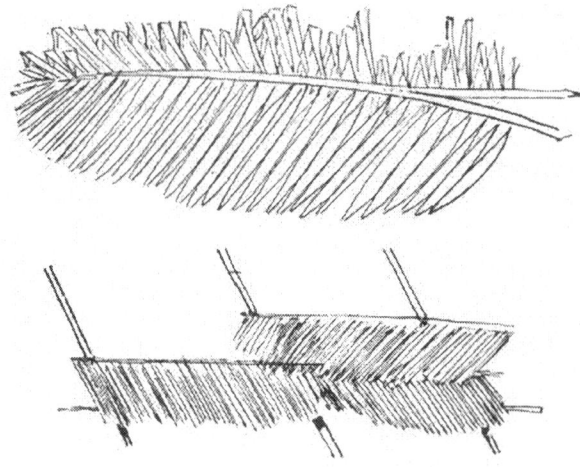

This thatch is particularly suitable for very long pinnate leaves. The centre rib of the palm frond is split. These split ribs are tied together and secured to the thatching battens with a good overlap. This method eliminates the need for thatching battens and is very efficient if suitable material is easily available.

Woven Thatch

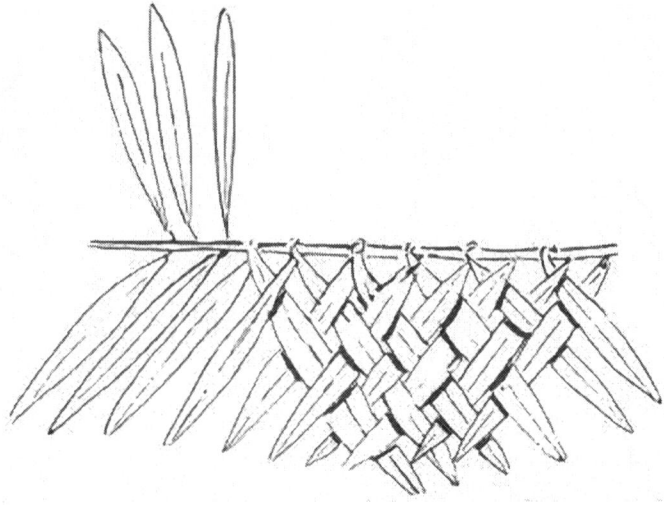

If time permits and the materials are readily available, an alternative method to the split stalk thatch is the woven thatch. The pinnate fronds are laid flat on the ground and the leaves from one side are laid over and woven between the leaves on the other side. The entire stalk is then tied on to the framework, observing the same principle of overlap which applies to the other methods.

Sewn Batten Thatch

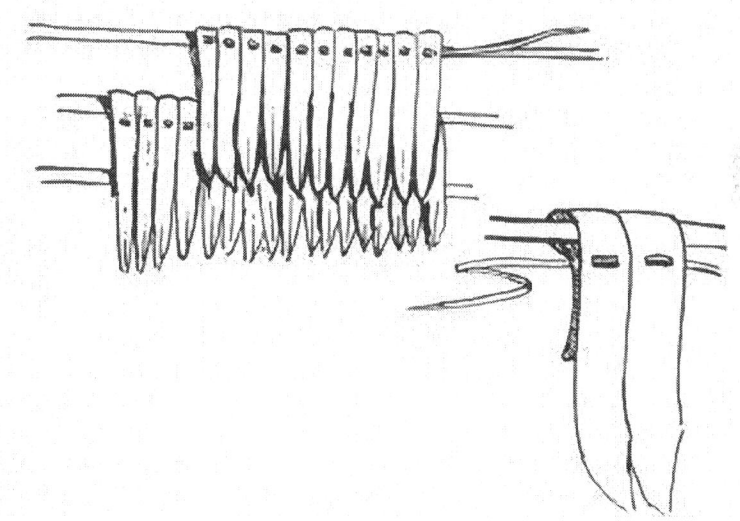

With other long, broad-leaved materials the leaves may be bent over sticks on the ground and a thin sliver of split cane or other suitable material used to sew the two sections of the leaves together. The sticks are then tied to the framework as for split stalk thatching. This method is very neat and efficient for certain materials. If green material is to be used make certain that it will not curl as it dries out. Many grass materials will curl into thin strips, and the thatch will be almost ineffective. Dead material is generally best.

Ridge Thatching

In thatching the ridge it is essential to cover the stitching of the topmost row of thatching. If this stitching is covered there will be complete protection. If it is inadequately covered there will be a leak along the ridge.

The ridge thatch therefore must curl completely

over the ridge pole or, better still, over a false ridge pole or, alternatively, it may stand up from the ridge and, if bound tightly, will make an efficient watershed. For pyramidal and circular huts this last is the most efficient method.

Sewn Ridge Thatching

With very long material two heavy poles may be slung on slings, so that they lie on either side and hold the outside edges of the ridge thatch material down.

Another method of thatching a ridge is to tie on two battens to the top of the topmost layer of thatching. The ends of the ridge thatching material sewn to these two battens must overhang the sewing of the topmost layer.

An alternative method is to sew the ridge material on to three poles, one of which acts as a false ridge, and the other two, which are sewn tightly, hang over the ridge some twelve or eighteen inches on either side of the centre pole. This ridge thatch material can be sewn on the ground in lengths of from six to twelve feet, and when the roof is ready for ridging these are laid over the actual ridge proper and the two side poles allowed to hang on either side, covering the top layer of stitching.

Crown Ridge Thatch

Guttering

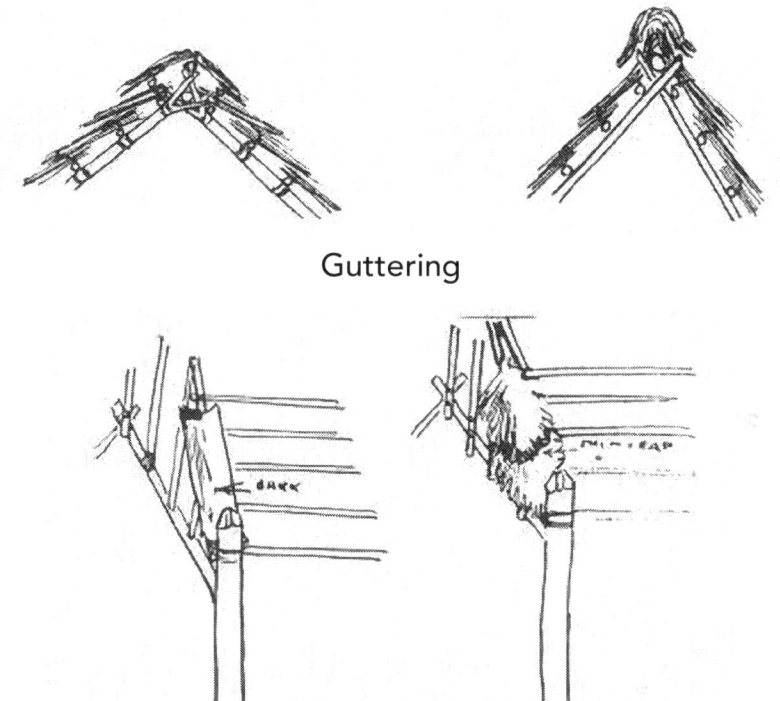

Under some conditions it may be necessary to put a "valley" in the roof, and this will require guttering. Efficient guttering can be made from wide sheets of bark inverted so that they lie with the hollow side in the valley. An alternative is the use of hollowed-out palm trunks or the extra-wide leaves of the plicate palms can be laid to overlap each other. Considerable care must be taken with this guttering if you are to have a watertight roof.

Flashing

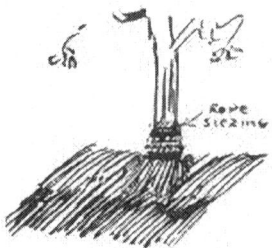

There are occasions when flashing may be required. For instance, there may be a tree growing through the roof where the ridge pole is held up, or for some reason some of the structural poles or tree trunks may project through the roof thatch. When flashing is required, simply spin up a length of thin rope from grass or other soft fibrous material (see the volume titled "Ropemaking") and bind thatching round the tree or pole. Continue the binding an inch or two above top of the thatching material. Make sure that it is tight and secure. The rain will run down the tree trunk, come to the flashing binding and, seeping over it, come on to the thatch, from where it is led by natural flow to the thatch of the roofing.

Rammed Earth

This method of building makes a permanent structure which is well insulated and low in cost. The only materials required for the walls are earth containing certain wide proportions of clay and sand or other gritty particles. The earth must also be free from organic materials such as grass, roots and the like.

Rammed earth buildings can either be built by erecting forms- or by ramming earth in blocks (like large bricks) and laying these in courses.

Foundations and footings are made by setting large stones in clay in the foundation trench. Clay is in many ways better than concrete for rammed earth buildings, because it is impervious to moisture.

If concrete foundations are used, then it is necessary to put in a dampcourse, but with clay and stone no dampcourse is needed.

- Photo by John Culliton

Foundations

The foundations (footings), as shown here, are large stones set in clay. The foundations extend from six to nine inches above ground level. Foundation trench is 2 ft. wide by 1 ft. deep, and lined with at least one inch of clay. After laying the stones in the clay, they are rammed to make a firm bed.

The advantage of this method of laying foundations is that there is no cost, and the method is speedy.

One man can dig and lay fifteen to twenty feet of foundation in a day.

The foundation must extend above ground level so that in the event of very heavy rain the surface run-off will not reach to the rammed earth wall.

Soil Qualities for Rammed Earth

Any "heavy" loamy soil is suitable for rammed earth building. The soil must be just right for its moisture content.

To find out the right "consistency", roll up a ball of the earth (about the size of a golfball) between the palms and drop it from a height of about one foot. If the ball breaks up, the soil is too dry, and moisture must be added before ramming.

If the ball does not break from a foot high drop, then hold the ball above the head and drop it again. If the ball does not shatter into small fragments with a six or seven foot drop, then the soil is too moist and must be allowed to dry out before ramming.

The qualities in the soil are easily determined. There should be not more than 70 per cent sand, and not less than 30 per cent. There should be not more than 70 per cent clay and silt, and not less than 30 per cent.

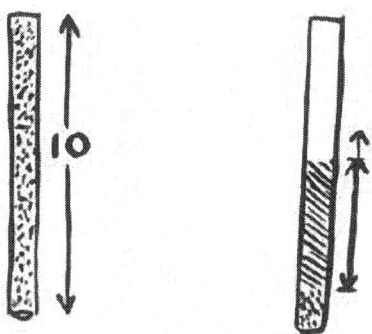

If Sand or Grit is between three-tenths and seven-tenths soil will be O.K.

To discover if the soil is all right for rammed earth work, take a glass tube ten inches long, or, alternatively, divide a glass tube into ten equal divisions. Dry some of the earth, crumble it to fine powder, and fill the tube. Take the exact quantity which was in the tube and put it into a billy or dish, and wash thoroughly in running water until all the clay and silt particles have been washed out. Dry the remainder and then put back into the tube. The level will tell you the approximate percentage of clayey content that was in the soil.

If the soil has too much clay it will crack; if too little clay or too much sand or organic matter it will crumble.

—Photo by John Culliton.

The photo above shows a rammed earth Hostel in course of erection. This hostel is to provide snow accommodation for 20 people. It is 35ft. by 22ft., 8ft. walls, 1ft. thick. The total cost of the building is estimated to be under £100. The only materials bought are iron for the roof, timber for roof, and floor, doors, windows, and 5 bags of cement for facing of the rammed earth wall and also for a 3-inch top sill for same.

Forms

Forms can be made and bolted together, and in these the earth can be rammed or, alternatively, moulds can be made and the earth rammed into these to form blocks, and these blocks are then laid in courses like large bricks.

If forms are used they need not be more than two or three feet high and six to eight feet long. The forms are held by bolts which, when tightened up, clamp the form to the wall.

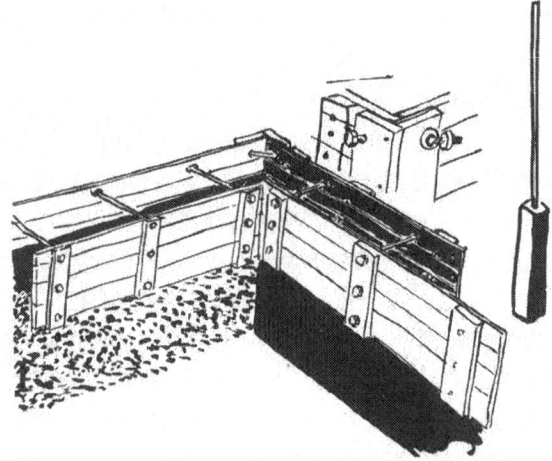

When ramming, shovel in three or four inches of earth and ram until the earth "rings". This is quite a definite sound, unmistakable from the soft "thud thud" of the first ramming strokes.

Ramming is hard work, and tiring.

When the layer is "ringing", throughout its length, shovel in another three or four inches of soil, and repeat.

Rammers should be from 6 to 8 lb. A hardwood base, about 4 in. x 4 in. x 10 in. long, handle maybe a 5 ft. length of gaspipe.

If moulds are used they must be of a design which can be quickly "knocked down" to remove the rammed earth block, and as quickly re-assembled.

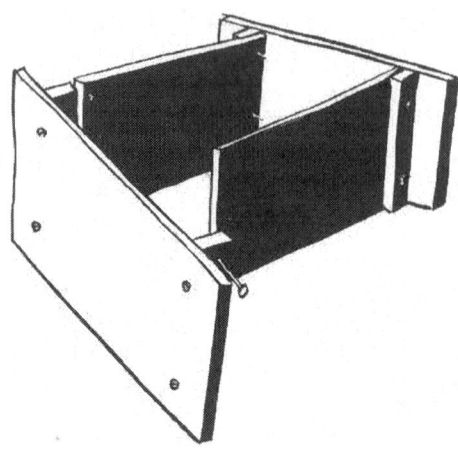

One man can fill and ram about nine to twelve cubic feet in a day.

Rammed earth walls should be at least nine to ten inches in thickness for an eight-foot wall, or twelve to fifteen inches if a top structure or greater height are required.

Rammed earth walls may be protected from driving rain either by providing a wide overhang to the eave, by plastering with a cement or lime mortar, or by giving a cement "skin" by brushing on a thick cement-sand mixture (one-to-two proportion). However, even without the cement skin, rammed earth will stand up to a hundred years or more of weather.

Log Cabins

Where timber is plentiful and white ants are not prevalent and a structure of permanence is required, the Log Cabin is suitable. It is permanent, solid, and easy to build. The construction is simple. Cut your logs (which should be of roughly uniform diameter) to within a few inches of the required lengths. Lay the bed logs, which should be the heaviest logs. See that these are laid square. Where the end logs lie across the back and front logs, halve or scarf the sites for the logs.

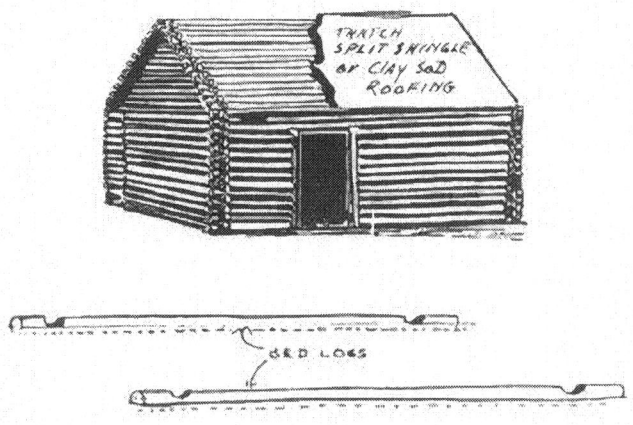

The remainder of the construction follows exactly the same method. The logs are carved into each other.

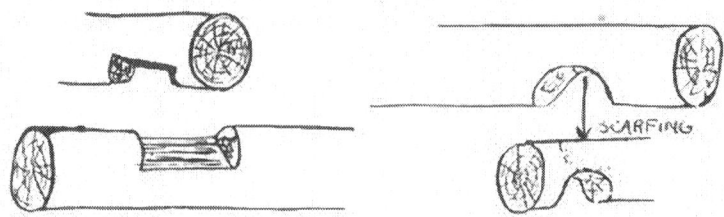

These are two methods of scarfing logs for building. The flat surface of the bottom log always "falls" outwards, so that when any rainwater blows in it will not find a place for easy lodgement, but will drain away because of the natural slope of the bottom of the scarf. Chinks between the logs should be filled with clay.

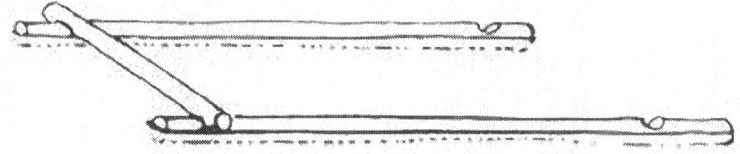

Materials for Lashings

In bushcraft work it is assumed that no manufactured materials are available, and therefore in hut making lashing must be used when no nails are available. Rope, too, may be unprocurable, and it is then necessary to know what natural materials can be used and how.

For lashing, sewing, and tying, any ground or tree vine which has length, strength and pliability will serve. Length, of course, is visible and easily found, but tests for strength and pliability should be applied. The test for strength is simply to exert a steady straight pull on the material. You will be able to judge its breaking strain if under sixty or eighty pounds. The test for pliability is to tie a thumb knot in the vine and gently pull the knot tight. If the vine snaps or cuts upon itself, it lacks pliability and must be discarded.

In addition to ground and tree vines, the outer skin of the long leaves of most palms may be used for ties. To harvest these, nick the hard outer shell with a cut about one-quarter inch wide and an eighth of an inch deep. Start the outer cane splitting, and to prevent it "running off" bend the thick portion away from the thin.

This is most important. If you pull the thin strip and bend it away from the main stalk, it will split for a few feet and then "run off." This principle of bending AWAY from the tendency to run off applies to all canes, palms, vines, bamboos and barks.

Barks

The inner bark of many shrubs and trees, alive or dead, also makes excellent lashing material. Strip down to the required thickness, but watch out for weak places.

Special Knots

Many of the sedges have length and strength and may be used for lashing and sewing work.

Nearly all the bulrushes can serve as lashings, and many of the "sword grasses" or sedges, but be careful handling these, as the razor-sharp edge can make nasty little cuts in your skin which poison easily. If handling any of the sword grasses, put a pair of socks on your hands and so save your skin.

Sedges and Bulrushes

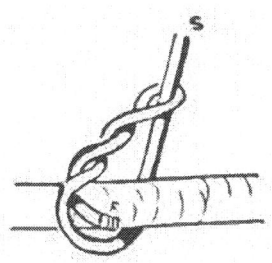

These green materials require special knots if they are to be used to best advantage. For example, the customary start of a square lashing is with a clove hitch (see also the handbook titled "Knots and Lashings"), but a clove hitch on "green" bush material is useless. The natural springiness in the material will cause the start of the knot to open. ALWAYS start a lashing with a timber hitch, as shown above.

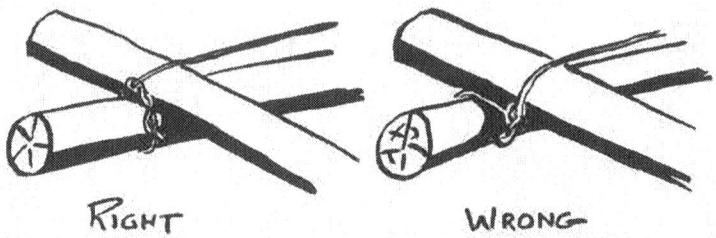

And ALWAYS see that the free end passes straight through the "eye" and does not come back against the eye. If it does, it will probably cut itself.

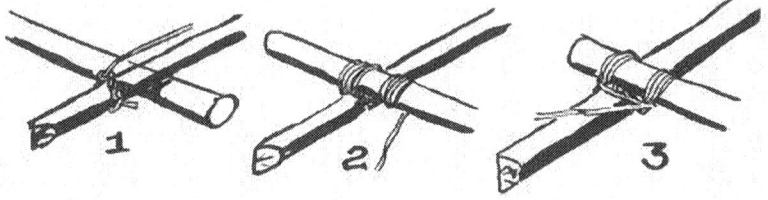

Start your lashing with a timber hitch, as Fig. 1; make three to six complete turns around the two poles, and "work" them together as you tighten the lashing at each turn (Fig. 2).

The trapping turns (Fig. 3) follow. These trapping turns close the lashing in, and tighten the whole job. Finish off by passing the free end of the material through an opening of the lashing and finish with a couple of half hitches pulled tight.

Joining Green Materials

An overhand knot (Fig. 1) will often serve, but if the material "cuts," try a sheet bend (Fig. 2) or a reef knot (Fig. 3). There are many ways of joining green materials either by plaiting or by spinning into rope. These are fully explained in the volumes titled "Bush Ropemaking" and "Knots and Lashings".

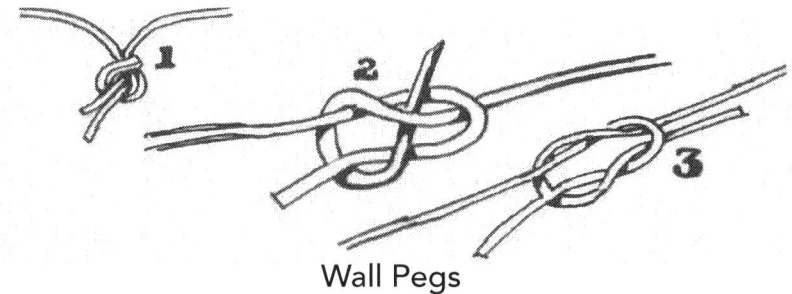

Wall Pegs

Wall pegs, and all stakes which are to be driven into the ground, must be straight, have the head bevelled and the foot pointed. Avoid pointing with a single cut.

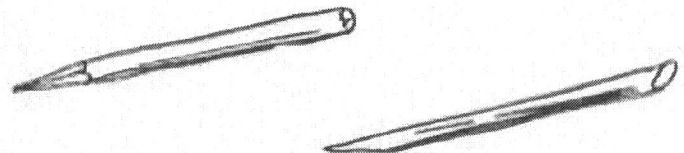

Made in the USA
Monee, IL
02 November 2019